For Sandy
—R.L.

For Maira & Dastan
—Yusup

Petunia the Unicorn's Magically Marvelous Ballet
Petunia the Unicorn® is a Registered Trademark of Waystation Media LLC

All rights reserved. This book or any portion thereof may not be reproduced or used in any manner whatsoever without the express written permission of the publisher except for the use of brief quotations in a book review.

Published by But That's Another Story... Press
Ridgefield, CT

Printed in the United States of America.

First Printing, 2022.

ISBN: 978-1-953713-24-7
Library of Congress Control Number: 2022914614

Petunia the Unicorn's
Magically Marvelous Ballet

A Petunia Cupcake Fluffybottom Book

Written by R.L. Ullman
Illustrations by Yusup Mediyan

But That's Another Story... Press

Hi, I'm Petunia. My full name is Petunia Cupcake Fluffybottom. I'm a unicorn!

This is my family. I live with my amazing Auntie Sprinkles, my spunky dog Gumdrop, and our dependable butler Winston. We live on West 81st Street in Manhattan.

I'm living in the human world for the very first time! It's been really exciting and I've tried lots of new things.

Trampolining…

Even jumping rope.

At bedtime, I ask Auntie Sprinkles if she thinks there's anything here I might be good at.
"Oh, darling," she says, "the point is to try new activities to see what you enjoy. No one is great at everything and that's okay. Just focus on having fun."

"Well, it sure would be nice to be good at something," I mutter.
"Hmm," Auntie Sprinkles says. "I know something you might like."

The next morning, Auntie Sprinkles tells me she's signed me up for ballet.
"What's ballet?" I ask.
"What's ballet, darling?" she says with surprise. "Why, it's simply the most elegant form of dance ever!"

"You'll learn to do arabesques, and pirouettes, and so much more! All Fluffybottoms are blessed with remarkable grace. Why, I'm sure you'll be a natural!"

After that, ballet is all Auntie Sprinkles can think about. She pliés while eating. Relevés while reading.

And grand jetés instead of walking.

Then, Auntie Sprinkles takes me shopping for a ballet outfit.
"You don't choose the tutu, dumpling," she says. "The tutu chooses you."

That night, I'm so excited for my first ballet class I can't sleep.

Since Auntie Sprinkles has a business appointment, Winston takes me to class at Madame Bumblebee's Ballet School. When we walk in, I feel like I have butterflies in my stomach.

Unfortunately, my dancing skills aren't as good as the other kids. I guess not all Fluffybottoms are blessed with remarkable grace.

And just in case I didn't know it, Madison, the best ballerina in class, tells me so.
"You're clumsy," she says.
"I've never done ballet before," I say.
"That's obvious," she says.

Before we leave, Madame Bumblebee says that we'll be performing a recital at the end of the session and anyone can audition for the lead role of the Princess Dove.

"I always get the lead role," Madison whispers to me. "But don't worry, I'm sure Madame Bumblebee will hide you in the back."

That night, Auntie Sprinkles asks me how ballet class went.
"I liked it," I say. "But I'm not very good."
"You mean, you're not very good *yet*," Auntie Sprinkles says. "If you practice, you'll get better and better."

Soon, I find myself practicing everywhere I go. I really like ballet, but I didn't like what Madison whispered to me.

At the next class, I do much better. Afterwards, Madame Bumblebee informs us that auditions will be next week.

"I'm going to be the Princess Dove," Madison says confidently. "You'll probably be a pigeon."

That week I work harder than I've ever worked before. Even Winston and Gumdrop get into it.

The night before auditions, I tell Auntie Sprinkles that I'm going to try out for the Princess Dove.
"Oh, how wonderful," she says.
"But Madison is really good," I say. "I'm sure she'll get the part."
"That's okay," Auntie Sprinkles says. "I'm just proud of you for putting yourself out there."

The next day is the audition and only Madison and I try out for the Princess Dove.
After Madison does a flawless routine, it's my turn.
I do my very best.

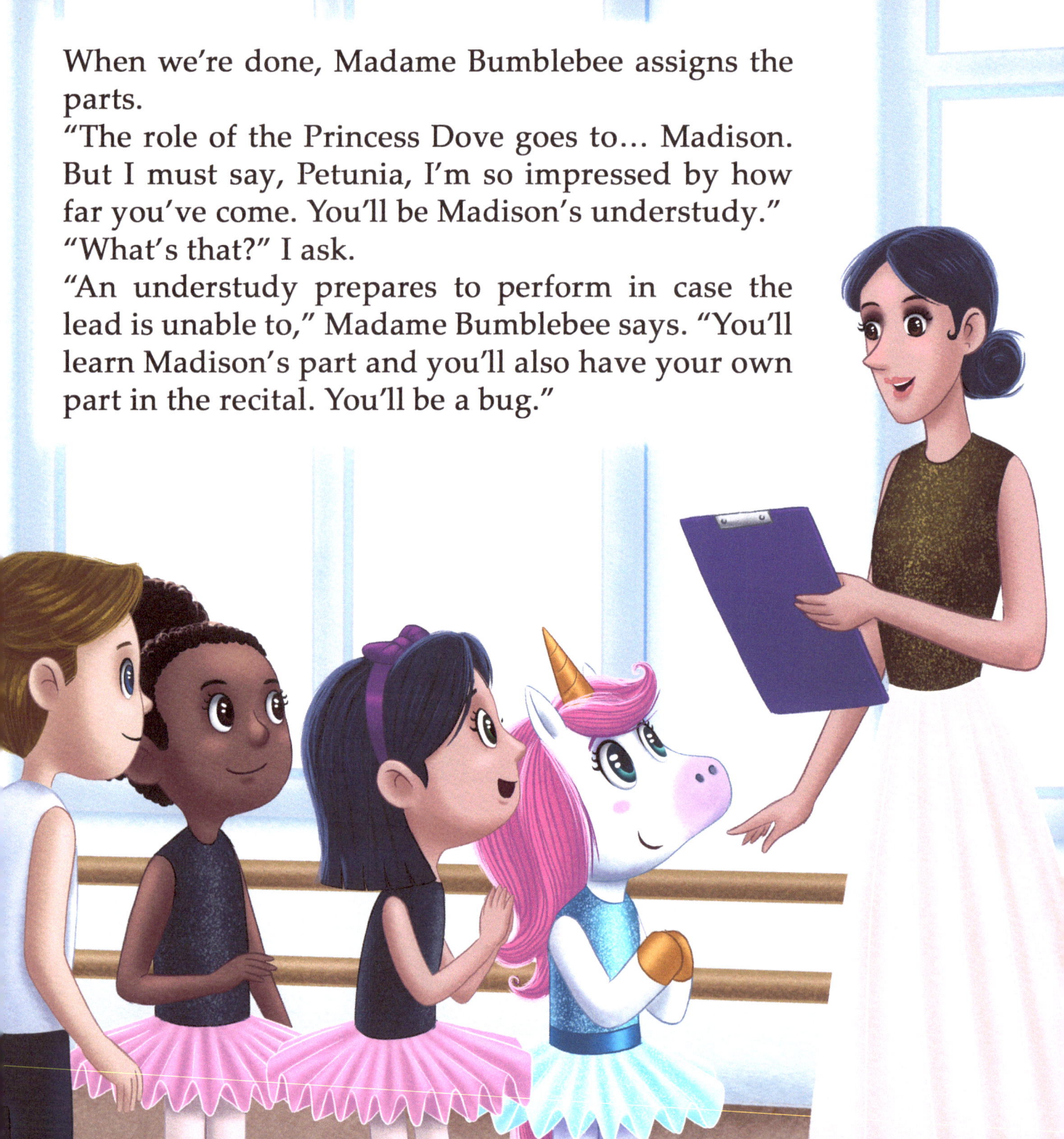

When we're done, Madame Bumblebee assigns the parts.

"The role of the Princess Dove goes to… Madison. But I must say, Petunia, I'm so impressed by how far you've come. You'll be Madison's understudy."

"What's that?" I ask.

"An understudy prepares to perform in case the lead is unable to," Madame Bumblebee says. "You'll learn Madison's part and you'll also have your own part in the recital. You'll be a bug."

"Congratulations," I say to Madison after class. "Your performance was beautiful."
"I know," she says. "You won't have to worry about being my understudy because nothing will stop me from being the Princess Dove."

After weeks of practice, it's finally time for the performance. As we're getting ready backstage, I'm shocked when I see Madison come in on crutches!

"Oh, no, Madison!" I exclaim. "What happened?"

"I tripped over my dog," Madison says with tears in her eyes. "Now I can't perform. But I'm sure you're happy because you get to be the Princess Dove."

But I don't feel happy.
"Madison, seeing you hurt doesn't make me happy," I say. "You should be the Princess Dove."
"But that's impossible," she says. "My leg is injured."
I think for a second and say, "I can fix that."

"My leg! It's healed!" Madison exclaims as she flexes it back and forth. "But... how did you do that?"
"With unicorn magic," I say.
"You did that for me?" Madison asks confused. "But... why?"
"Because you're a great ballerina," I say. "I really enjoy watching you and I know the audience will too."

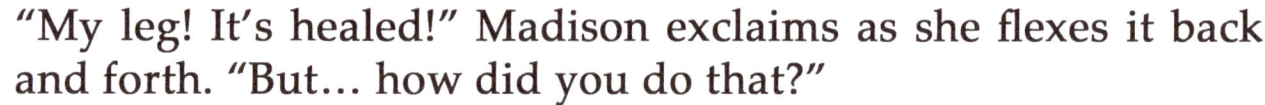

Madison danced beautifully and I had lots of fun. Afterwards, Madison finds me backstage.
"Petunia, I'm so sorry I wasn't nice to you," she says. "You're a great ballerina and an even better friend."
"Gee, thanks," I say.
"Do you want to come over tomorrow?" Madison asks. "We can dance for our dogs and this time you can be the Princess Dove."
"That sounds like fun!" I say. "I'd like that."

And that's exactly what we did.

R.L. Ullman is the bestselling author of award-winning books for kids. He creates fun, engaging stories that kids (and adults) want to read. R.L. lives with his wife, son, two dogs, and a laptop in Connecticut. Find out what R.L. is up to at rlullman.com.

Yusup Mediyan is a freelance illustrator and animator who lives in West Java, Indonesia. He has illustrated children's books, book covers, and several animated series. He is also a father of two.

Reviews are important to bring this book to the attention of more readers. So, if you enjoyed this book, we would be very grateful if you could leave an honest review online. Thanks for your support!

Printed in the USA
CPSIA information can be obtained
at www.ICGtesting.com
LVHW061702191223
766720LV00020B/1349